THE DOUBLE ANNOINTING OF ELISHA

By
MICHAEL ADIKWU

PUBLISHED by PARABLES
Earthly Stones with a Heavenly Meaning

The Double Anointing of Elisha
Michael Adikwu

Published By Parables
July, 2020

All Rights Reserved. No part of this book may be reproduced or utilized in any form or by any means, electronic or mechanical, including photocopying, recording, or by any information storage and retrieval system, without permission in writing from the author.

> ISBN 978-1-951497-73-6
> Printed in the United States of America

Readers should be aware that Internet Web sites offered as citations and/or sources for further information may have been changed or disappeared between the time this was written and the time it is read.

THE DOUBLE ANNOINTING OF ELISHA
BY
MICHAEL ADIKWU

PUBLISHED by PARABLES
Earthly Stories with a Heavenly Meaning

Dedication

To the Holy Ghost for His influence upon my life over the years and to my late father, Mr. Matthew Adikwu Okodo, who blessed me before his death.

Michael Adikwu

About the Book

Those that God uses, He anoints. God had instructed Elijah to anoint his servant, Elisha. Elisha had worked with his master for some time. He knew that his master, Elijah had chosen even to die to escape the terrible problem in the land of Israel. The nation had become very idolatrous and Elijah had killed 450 prophets of Baal on Mount Carmel. He was, however, afraid of going further after hearing the threats of Jezebel, although he was at the verge of bringing revival to the land of Israel. To be able to replace such a man would require double the amount of anointing he was having. Elisha, therefore, asked for double his anointing. He was given conditions, which he was able to fulfill and actually received this double anointing. He, however, was not able to use his double anointing for the purpose for which it was meant but concentrated on miracles. God has placed a sword in his hands with that anointing but, unfortunately, his anointing was misplaced. Thank God that he knew the man who could do the job, an army man, Jehu. Jehu executed the job to the satisfaction of Heaven that God even commended him (2 Kings 10:30). If a double anointing of Elijah's anointing was not sufficient for Elisha, what amount of anointing do we need in our generation that has degenerated very terribly? That is the purpose for this book.

The Double Anointing of Elisha

Purpose

Those that God uses, He anoints. God had instructed Elijah to anoint his servant, Elisha. Elisha had worked with his master for some time. He knew that his master, Elijah had chosen even to die to escape the terrible problem in the land of Israel.

The nation had become very idolatrous and Elijah had killed 450 prophets of Baal on Mount Carmel. He was, however, afraid of going further after hearing the threats of Jezebel, although he was at the verge of bringing revival to the land of Israel.

To be able to replace such a man would require double the amount of anointing he was having. Elisha, therefore, asked for double his anointing. He was given conditions, which he was able to fulfill and actually received this double anointing. He, however, was not able to use his double anointing for the purpose for which it was meant but concentrated on miracles.

God has placed a sword in his hands with that anointing but, unfortunately, his anointing was misplaced. Thank God that he knew the man who could do the job, an army man, Jehu. Jehu executed the job to the satisfaction of Heaven that God even commended him (2 Kings 10:30). If a double anointing of Elijah's anointing was not sufficient for Elisha, what amount of anointing do we need in our generation that has degenerated very terribly? That is the purpose for this book.

Chapter One: Introduction
The Problem with Israel

Israel is a country or nation we need to learn a lot from. The Israeli walk with God is like the life of every Christian - up and down. When the Israelites came back to the Promised Land their rebellion multiplied against God. It was not as if they were very alright when their leaders such as Moses and Joshua were alive. On their journey to the Promised Land, they rebelled several times in the desert. As a result of that, their journey that was to take only three days now took forty years. In fact, God was very much aware of their nature – that they were a rebellious people and would simply return if they encounter problems on the way. Look at God's instruction to Moses.

"When Pharaoh let the people go, God did not lead them on the road through the Philistine country, though that was shorter. For God said, "If they face war, they might change their minds and return to Egypt" (Exodus 3:17).

Thus, they were meant to follow a zig-zag road that was to last for forty days. The forty days eventually turned to be forty years. I said that our current life is like that of the Israelites because even Moses the man of God failed at a point. It was not just the rebellion of the children of Israel but that of their leader also became a serious matter. God had instructed Moses to go and speak to the rock. Instead of speaking to the rock, Moses struck the rock. This might be because Moses had just lost his sister Miriam and the sorrow was still in his heart (Numbers

20:1-8). You can imagine people, instead of being sorrowful and commiserating with you, they chose to put pressure on you to get water for them. Secondly, most of us are usually stuck to our old methods. God is not routine. There are pastors who must always use anointing oil not knowing that God is never routine. God wants to fellowship with us and He is ready to give us instructions every time. When He gives an instruction, he does not expect you to deviate from it for a moment. In an earlier instruction, God had told Moses to strike the rock. Now again, Moses struck the rock for the second time. Water still came out, but what followed was that Moses would not be able to see the Promised Land. In Deuteronomy 3:23-26 he said he prayed about it three times, but God warned him never to pray about that again! He was very eager to reach the Promised Land. Before he died, God instructed him to climb Mount Pisgah so that he could catch a glimpse of the Promised Land (Deuteronomy 3:27). Reaching there was out of the question.

Yes, Moses struck the Rock in disobedience but water however came out for the people to drink. Why many people will go to hell is because they are following methods that work! That you placed anointing oil on the head of a member of the congregation and he tumbled "under anointing" does not mean it is the will of God. That is why many people are being deceived today with anointing oil and holy water and handkerchiefs. If God has not instructed a thing and you keep doing it because you are getting results, without God instructing you; be careful. The Bible said that the rock that followed them was Jesus Christ.

"Then Moses raised his arm and struck the rock twice with his staff. Water gushed out, and the community and their livestock drank" (Numbers 20:11).

"And drank the same spiritual drink; for they drank from the spiritual rock that accompanied

them, and that rock was Christ" (1 Corinthians 10:4).

If that rock that followed them was Jesus Christ, then Moses broke an eternal law because Jesus was to be struck once and not twice. Jesus came to die for the world once and will not come to die again.

If you read your Bible very well, God called Moses to the mountain in Exodus 24:12:

"The Lord said to Moses, "Come up to me on the mountain and stay here, and I will give you the tablets of stone with the law and commandments I have written for their instruction."

Moses was on the mountain for 40 good days. God was instructing him on ministerial methods. The patterns of how to run the priestly office and the type of garments for the priests were clearly given to him (Exodus 28:2).

He was also shown how the Ark of the Covenant was to be shaped and those to do the work (Exodus 31:1-7). This started from Exodus Chapter 24 to 32, eight whole chapters. When the children of Israel made a calf in Chapter 32, God at that time told Moses to go down and see how the people had become perverted (Exodus 32:7).

"Then the Lord said to Moses, "Go down, because your people,

whom you brought up out of Egypt, have become corrupt. They have been quick to turn away from what I commanded them and have made themselves an idol cast in the shape of a calf. They have bowed down to it and sacrificed to it and have said, 'These are your gods, Israel, who brought you up out of Egypt.'"

When Moses came down he was very angry to the extent that he broke the Ten

Commandments and all the other stories that followed. He sort of made an altar call (Exodus 32:27-29):

"Then he said to them, "This is what the Lord, the God of Israel, says: 'Each man strap a sword to his side. Go back and forth through the camp from one end to the other, each killing his brother and friend and neighbor.'" The Levites did as Moses commanded, and that day about three thousand of

the people died. Then Moses said, "You have been set apart to the Lord today, for you were against your own sons and brothers, and he has blessed you this day."

Now after this God called Moses back to the mountain. This ended in about one to two chapters. Moses was to cut the stones by himself for his excessive anger. God was teaching him personnel attributes of how not to be "over" angry. He was on the mountain for forty days as in the first case, but God was teaching him about his personal life and not about ministry. After all, he was taken from following sheep which were not intelligent animals. He should not be annoyed to the extent of striking the rock instead of speaking to it because of the children of Israel. That should also teach everyone a lesson.

The people that will make you to miss heaven are

members of your household or members of your congregation; if you do not take heed. God was unequivocal with Moses about this (Exodus 34:12). **"Take heed to thyself…"** Everyone must take heed to himself or herself in this journey to heaven.

Let's Learn from David

We must take heed too to hear God on every matter. Do not say God told me before. No. What God told you yesterday will not suffice for today. The Bible says, David was a man after God's heart (1 Samuel 13:14).

"But now thy kingdom shall not continue: the Lord hath sought him a man after his own heart, and the Lord hath commanded him to be captain over his people, because thou hast not kept that which the Lord commanded thee."

David never relied on what God told him in the past. If

The Double Anointing of Elisha

David is going to war in the morning he will ask God. "Should I go?" God will say, "Go". "Will I win?" God will say, "You will win." He will ask again, "How do I attack?" God will say, "From the back of the mountain." That was his life style. How I wish we have such pastors today. Even when his family and those of the soldiers were all captured and taken away in Ziklag, he had to be asking these questions even when his followers were ready to stone him! (1 Samuel 30:3-10). We should never use what God told us yesterday as the basis for judging today's events. Do not use your past experiences for future judgments. While testimonies are good, they are like the ashes of Leviticus 6: 12. Ashes obtained after they have burnt the wood or the grass are no longer effective for roasting or cooking anything. Remember that

The Double Anointing of Elisha

when Jesus was on the earth, He never repeated the same miracles in the same manner. He healed the blind three times using different methods. On one occasion, He just told the blind to begin to see, and the person began to see. The other He robbed saliva on the eyes and the person began to "see men like trees." He repeated it and the man began to see well. The third person, He told him to go and wash in the Pool of

Siloam. After this the man began to see.

God wants to fellowship with us more than anything else. He did not tell His disciples any formula they could use if they met the blind or hunch-backed or any form of diseased person. Look at His promise, I am with you always even to the end of the age (Matthew 28:20). That is the method of God always being with His people. He told Moses, He would be with him (Exodus 3:12).

"And God said, "I will be with you. And this will be the sign to you that it is I who have sent you: When you have brought the people out of Egypt, you will worship God on this mountain."

God never wants to leave us alone. The only condition that makes God to leave us is sin. When Moses was no longer in the scene, He told

Joshua, "As I was with Moses, so I will be with you" (Joshua 1:5). God created us to fellowship with him. Even the people Jesus chose as His disciples, this fellowship was uppermost in His mind. Look at Mark 3:14; the King James Version puts it more succinctly;

"And he ordained twelve, that they should be with him, and that he might send them forth to preach,"

Being with Him is a "should" while their going to preach is a "might." God wants our fellowship. In fact, what will you preach when you have not been with him in the secret place? It is what He teaches you that makes you an effective preacher. Remember the story of Mary and Martha? (Luke 10: 41-42)

"But one thing is needed, and Mary has chosen that good part, which will not be taken away from her."

Yes, being with Jesus and listening to him is more important than any other thing else that one choses, including cooking of food to entertain our Lord. You need to listen to Jesus daily and do not take what He told you yesterday as the message for today. Acting that way has ended the life of many men of God. Moses lost the Promised Land to that kind of life. Water still issued out for the children of Israel to drink but Moses' journey was reconfigured negatively. The language of many people today is, "it is working." It is working, but is it of God? Do you remember the bronze snake that Moses made in the desert when the children of Israel sinned and snakes were everywhere on them? The children of Israel kept it because it was working. It was King Hezekiah that burnt it (2 Kings 18:4) and that pleased God. I am sure they kept it because it was working.

"He removed the high places, smashed the sacred stones and cut down the Asherah poles. He broke into pieces the bronze snake Moses had made, for up to that time the Israelites had been burning incense to it. (It was called Nehushtan)."

Yes, many things that many pastors and others are using

today are working but they are not of God.

Moses Valedictory Speech in the Desert

The book of Deuteronomy was the valedictory speech of Moses. He had told them of all the blessings and all the curses that would follow them. Some of the curses were so frightful and because of lack of space, we need to just read Deuteronomy 28. Just few verses (about 14 of them) were devoted to the blessings and the remaining portion of a very long chapter is devoted to the curses. The question is whether the children of Israel obeyed these injunctions. In Deuteronomy 30: 19, Moses was very unequivocal:

"I call heaven and earth to record this day against you, that I have set before you life and death, blessing and cursing: therefore choose life, that both thou and thy seed may live."

That was a clear message to the children of Israel. And this did not stop here. Before the death of Joshua he also gave his valedictory injunction.

And if it seem evil unto you to serve the Lord, choose you this day whom ye will serve; whether the gods which your fathers served that were on the other side of the flood, or the gods of the Amorites, in whose land ye dwell: but as for me and my

house, we will serve the Lord (Joshua 24:15).

After the death of Joshua and the elders that followed, the children of Israel forgot what they were told all along the way and what gave them success in the battle for the Promised Land. The Bible declares in Judges 21: 25:

"In those days Israel had no king; everyone did as they saw fit."

The Double Anointing of Elisha

You can imagine a people without a king. Who will organize the people in case of battle? In fact, who would even tell them about God? As such 2 Chronicles 15:3 says:

"For a long time Israel was without the true God, without a priest to teach and without the law."

When there are no kings, who would organize the priests and even make them to know the laws of God?

Such was the trouble in the land and such is the trouble that is plaguing the church and Christians in this our time. Today, genuine men of God are becoming rare. People are being confused left, right and centre. There is a lack of "Shall I pursue after this troop? Shall I overtake them?" God's Vineyard workers are no longer keen on hearing God say, "Pursue: for thou shalt surely overtake them, and without fail recover all" (1

Samuel 30:8-KJV). Dependence on tools of yesterday; reliance on methods of the past and stale testimonies now pervade sermons and the way we live our Christian lives. There is the need to go back to the basics: man having *koinonia* with GOD, as He originally intended. That is the purpose of this booklet.

Michael Adikwu

Chapter Two:
The Reason why Elijah was Raised

Elijah was raised to confront the gods of the land. Ahab the son of Omri the king of Israel had married a demonic woman called Jezebel. Ahab became king of Israel in the thirty-eighth year of Asa, king of Judah, and reigned for twenty-two years. In his 22 year reign his wicked wife was largely in charge. Jezebel was a Phoenician woman and came to be queen with the gods of Phoenicia. There are people today who think they can marry anyhow. Your journey with God will not go far. It was the evil activity of this king and queen that eventually paved the for prophet Elijah to emerge. The queen corrupted the land with her prophets of Baal.

To show that God was more powerful than their gods, particularly Baal, Elijah went and proclaimed to the king that there would be no dew nor rain unless by his (Elijah's) words (1 Kings 18:1). The type of draught was such that even dew refused to fall.

God Tests Elijah

For many men of God, they preach that they are kings and as such would not face any test. God does not use a man He has not tested. Even for Jesus, when He saw the multitude (John 6:5-6), He asked Philip,

"When Jesus looked up and saw a great crowd coming toward him, he said to Philip, "Where shall we buy bread for these people to eat?" He asked this only to test him, for he already had in mind what he was going to do."

Look at verse 6; it said, "He did this to test him." After all, Philip had said in John 1:45,

"*Philip found Nathanael and told him, "We have found the one Moses wrote about in the Law, and about whom the prophets also wrote—Jesus of Nazareth, the son of Joseph."*

If Philip believed this then he should be able to trust Jesus that He should be able to feed the multitude because that was what Moses wrote about Him. We could see Philip faltering here. Yes, God usually tests any man He wants to use.

The first test that came to Elijah was for him to go and hide. Should a man of God be willing to hide from a mere man? God, however, told him to go and hide (1 Kings 17:3). Today's men of God will doubt and will wonder if this was the voice of God and will keep binding and casting. Elijah was,

The Double Anointing of Elisha

however, sure it was the voice of God. Every man of God should be aware of how God speaks to him or her. Elijah went and hid. In addition, the voice of God told him that ravens would feed him! Ravens were unclean birds according to the Levitical laws, and if the touch any food, a man of God should not agree to eat it! Again Elijah was sure it was the voice of God and he agreed to eat the food from the ravens.

The next test was that after a while, the brook Cherith dried up (1 Kings 17: 7). If God had told him to drink from the brook why would it dry up? That was the next test. Today's pastors will begin to bind and cast out the demons leading to the drying of the brook thinking it is anti-God. Elijah did not do that. He obeyed the voice of God that told him to go and dwell with a widow at Zarephath (1 Kings 17:8-13). Remember that this was a young widow. Pastors of these days will just impregnate the widow and then try to justify their actions. Elijah, however, was steadfast. God, on seeing that he has passed all the tests, now told him to go and show himself to Ahab (1 Kings 18:1). God was sort of saying, "I can now trust this man all round!" God would not want to follow or use a man that would let Him down half way. You man of God, learn from men such as this.

Do not say, "He has extra grace". God's grace is available to us all, equally, teaching all to avoid ungodliness and worldly lust (Titus 2:11, 12). In fact, James would say (James 2:17):

"Elijah was a man with a nature like ours, and he prayed earnestly that it would not rain; and it did not rain on the land for three years and six months."

This is because we hear of terrible things by men of God of nowadays. No man of God will escape the wrath of God because we are surrounded by a crowd of witnesses (Hebrews 12:1)

The Battle of Elijah with the Prophets of Baal

The climax of Elijah's ministry was the battle with the prophets of Baal. When God had tested Elijah and did not find him wanting, He now told him to show himself to Ahab. It is the same God that told him to hide from Ahab that also told him to show himself to him. God seems to be saying, "I can now trust this man." On seeing him, Ahab shouted, "Is that you, you troubler of Israel?" (1 Kings 18:17). And Elijah quickly replied him (1 Kings 18:8),

"I have not made trouble for Israel," Elijah replied.

The Double Anointing of Elisha

"But you and your father's family have. You have abandoned the LORD's commands and have followed the Baals."

Remember that Omri the father of Ahab was a friend to the king of Phoenicia as stated in the introduction of this chapter. From this statement, it seems that the worship of Baal had been established even before Ahab had become king. That is how many fathers buy trouble for their children. The world is upside down today because many parents have not taken care of their children very well.

Elijah, therefore, confronted Ahab with the problem of the nation. The problem was not the draught in the land but the cause of the draught, the worship of Baal by the king and his family to the extent that they have 450 prophets of Baal. Remember that the prophets of Baal can prophesy! And the prophecies may be accurate. It is not every prophet of nowadays that is a genuine prophet of God. Look at the challenge posed by Elijah (1 Kings 18:19).

"Now summon the people from all over Israel to meet me on Mount Carmel. And bring the four hundred and fifty prophets of Baal and the four hundred prophets of Asherah, who eat at Jezebel's table."

Apart from the 450 prophets of Baal, there were also another 400 that were prophets of Asherah. There are nations today who have strange prophets and that is why diseases like Covid-19 is so hard on them.

And then comes the final aspect of the challenge (1 Kings 18:21, 23-24):

"***Elijah went before the people and said, "How long will you waver between two opinions? If*** *the Lord is God, follow him; but if Baal is God, follow him. And the people said nothing"*

"Get two bulls for us. Let Baal's prophets choose one for themselves, and let them cut it into pieces and put it on the wood but not set fire to it. I will prepare the other bull and put it on the wood but not set fire to it. Then you call on the name of your god, and I will call on the name of the Lord. The god who

answers by fire—he is God." Then all the people said, "What you say is good."

I have read history of some Christians who have challenged Islamic and other pagan nations in this manner. When the Name of the Lord is being toyed with, He will prevent any other God from doing any miracle. The prophets of Baal tried from morning till evening without any fire coming down. Then from the time of the evening sacrifice, Elijah took over. The Bible recorded that he repaired the altar on Mount Carmel. There are people who have destroyed the altar of their lives with sin and yet the claim they are still serving God. Some people have turned God's house into a business centre just because they perform miracles. When it matters most, their fire will not fall. Many today are touching

God's glory without fear. They need to be careful.

When Elijah had prepared the altar and with a short prayer, "Lord I have done this at thy word," the fire came down from heaven. Look at the things that were on the altar (1 Kings 18:38):

"Then the fire of the Lord fell and burned up the sacrifice, the wood, the stones and the soil, and also licked up the water in the trench."

When the altar of your life is correct there is nothing that will be too difficult to dissolve. Stones, soil and water are not combustible things. The fire that came down consumed all. God really does the impossible. If the prophets of Baal could call even fire down without the fire not consuming anything, one could have said they tried. No fire, however, came down. If Elijah had called fire down without it consuming all the things, he should have still be hailed. This fire that came down, however, did the impossible. The problem of the earth is not God but man. Nothing is too difficult for Him to do. All that He requires is the correct vessel to use. And so this battle was won and what followed was the rain that had not fallen for three years. It fell for the first time in three years of famine, that resulted in the death of most livestock. The revival of Israel had commenced.

Elijah Gives Up

But Jezebel sent a fiery message to Elijah (1Kings 19:2).

"May the gods deal with me, be it ever so severely, if by this time tomorrow I do not make your life like that of one of them."

Immediately Elijah's heart began to fail him. That is how the devil destroys our ways to big progress. For Elijah, it was the threat from Jezebel. For others, it might come in a different way. For Jesus, it was after 40 days of fasting that the devil came. He conquered the devil. For others, it is the love of money. For others it may be women. Unfortunately, the fiery prophet of God who could call down fire began to run away and even seeking to die. God asked what he was doing there running away from a woman. For God, He does not force anyone. God told Elijah to meet Him on Mount Horeb (1 Kings 19:9). In our generation, there are many people that God has tried in various ways for them to bring revival to the earth but unfortunately they went the way of Elijah. Why was God calling Elijah to Mount Horeb? Probably he wanted him to have a clearer view of the land more than he saw on Mount Carmel. Elijah refused to change his mind. That was at the verge of a mighty revival. God simply told him to retire to the desert of Damascus (1 Kings 19:15-16). In addition, he was to anoint Hazael as king of Syria, Jehu as King of Israel, and Elisha as prophet is his place. That was how Elijah the "mighty" man of God was retired from ministry by God Himself. Whether Elijah anointed those he was instructed to anoint or not, is a question that is beyond this booklet.

And let me add that Elijah's anointing did not diminish though he quickly gave up the fight against the "godless" people of the nation. He could still call fire down upon people and the people could just perish (2 Kings 1:10).

Michael Adikwu

Chapter Three: Elisha asks for Double Anointing

After these events, Elijah found Elisha ploughing in the field and from thence Elisha became his servant. Elisha show the enormity of the problem in the land of Israel. Elisha spent about 14 years with his master, and when it was time for his master to be taken away he asked for a double anointing. He was there with Elijah when he called fire down on the two captains and their fifties (2 Kings 1:10). He saw all the miracles that his boss had done. He thought aright when he asked for a double portion. In other words, "if you have this much anointing, yet you gave up, if I have the same amount of anointing, I will be left helpless." Of course, he got what he wanted. His master simply asked him to be attentive to be able to see him when he would be taken away from the earth.

Many of us are not able to receive much from God because we do not concentrate on watching to see what God would do to us. Many of us that are Christians concentrate more on our daily chores either at home or in the office more than on the things of God. Yet we go to church and with a sonorous voice sing, "I surrender all…" God will only use a man whose attention is on heavenly things more than on earthly cares. Jesus would tell His disciples,

"But seek ye first the kingdom of God, and his righteousness; and all these things shall be added unto you" (Matthew 6:33).

Unfortunately, what we actually do is to seek all other things first and then add heavenly matters as an addendum.

Yes, Elisha got his double anointing but the questions is, what did he do with it?

Elisha's Anointing Concentrated on Miracles

When Elijah and Elisha crossed the Jordan, his master asked what he wanted him to do for him (2 Kings 2:9). This was probably because, if he does not get anointing from him, how would he go back? After all they were able to cross the river because he, Elijah, struck the water with his mantle, which parted for them to cross. As such when Elisha saw Elijah being taken away the mantle he was wearing fell to the ground and he picked it. That guaranteed his return. When he thus came back to River Jordan, he too experimentally struck the river after shouting, "where is the Lord God of Elijah (2 Kings 2: 11). In fact, on returning to the city, some people of the city of Jericho complained to him about the

The Double Anointing of Elisha

city (2 Kings 2:19-20). They informed him that while the city looked beautiful, the water and other things in the land were not pleasant. He asked them to give him a cruse with salt in it. He went to the river and poured it and the condition of the city changed. Similarly, some 42 children were mocking him because of his bald head. He commanded two she bears and they tore them into pieces (2 Kings 2: 23-24). He could make an iron axe head to float (2 Kings 6:6). And the story of the miracles continued. He performed 14 notable miracles double that of his master Elijah. He was in fact a national prophet. The questions is, was that why he was anointed? Elisha was anointed to continue with the fight of his master Elijah. You can see that instead of doing this, from the time he got his anointing, he focused on miracles.

God Gives a Sword to His Followers

Look at the words that God Himself used to commission Elisha into ministry.

"Jehu will put to death any who escape the sword of Hazael, and Elisha will put to death any who escape the sword of Jehu" (1 Kings 19:17).

For every man that God commissions, he puts a sword in his hands. Elisha was permitted to use this sword, but he never did. He concentrated on one miracle or the other. Miracle is not the main thing. Miracles are useful but they are just an "addendum." In Nigerian parlance, miracles are like *"jiara."* When you have bought the main thing then you ask for it. It is given free usually in unmeasured amount. The main thing everyone should have is the anointing that saves souls. Yes, Elisha could do any type of miracle ranging from making iron to float to raising someone from the dead but that was not why he was anointed by God. Remember, he asked for double anointing. Elijah had just a "single" anointing and Elisha got the double of it yet, he never used it. Two things could be responsible for this: either he was too concentrated on his miracles that he forgot the main job or he just found out that his double anointing was useless when compared to the problem in the land. And I want to go for the second reason. That was why he chose to anoint Jehu thinking that he might have a better approach; the approach of a soldier man. Soldiers are usually militant in their behaviours.

In the Old Testament use of physical killing as a way of purging the land was permitted. That is not the case with the New

Testament. Before Jesus went to the cross, He asked His disciples to get a sword (Luke 22:36). Peter used this sword when Jesus was arrested and he cut off the ear lobe of Malchus and Jesus placed the ear lobe back (John 18:10). Jesus was demonstrating that the use of carnal weapons of warfare was ended that day He went to the cross. The Bible tells us that the weapons of our warfare are not carnal but mighty through God (2 Corinthians 10:3-5). Yes, for every man that is an obedient child of God, He gives him a sword to slay souls for Him; for the kingdom. This sword in our generation is the word of God. The Bible tells us that (Hebrews 4:12):

"For the word of God is alive and active. Sharper than any double-edged sword, it penetrates even to dividing soul and spirit, joints and marrow; it

judges the thoughts and attitudes of the heart."

That is the nature of the word of God. It has much more power than atomic bomb. It cannot be frustrated. God even said it cannot return to Him void (Isaiah 55:11). It must achieve what it was sent out to do. What can make the word of God not be active in the hand of a man is that the obedience of that man is not complete as recorded in 2

Corinthians 10:6. There is nothing that is difficult for the word of God. It is the sword of the spirit (Ephesians 6:17). No sickness can stand before it. No stubborn soul can withstand it when it is being used by the man whose obedience is complete. It can reach where drugs cannot reach. It is the drug for demon possession. But its most important function is that it is used is to slay souls for the kingdom.

The Double Anointing of Elisha

In the Old Testament, prophets were permitted to cleanse the land through physical killing. That was why Elisha was anointed. I see Elisha saying, "if I had known, I would have asked for more than this amount of anointing." I want also to thank God for his life as he knew what to do. He sent and anointed Jehu (2 Kings 9: 1-10), which his master, Elijah, did not do before he was taken from the earth. When Jehu was anointed, he did not waste time to begin the cleansing of the land. He started straight from Joram, followed by Jezebel and then the seventy sons of Ahab (2 Kings 9: 23-24; 2 Kings 10: 7). He wiped all of them out. Today, if you hear that Elisha is coming to town for crusade, what do you think will happen? The road to the venue of the crusade will be jam-packed because people will over-flow with cars and the crippled, the blind, the hunch-backed will be everywhere. If there is an announcement that Jehu is coming to hold a crusade, what do you think will happen? The venue will be empty. Look at God's testimony about Jehu (2 Kings 10:30):

"The Lord said to Jehu, "Because you have done well in accomplishing what is right in my eyes and have done to the house of Ahab all I had in

mind to do, your descendants will sit on the throne of Israel to the fourth generation."

Man of God, are you carrying out your ministry the way God wants it or you are busy prophesying and giving yourself big names? That was God testifying about Jehu, yet he did not do any recorded miracle in the Bible. No such testimony is available for Elisha. Beware lest the master should say on the last day (Matthew 7:21), "I never knew you,"

"Not everyone who says to me, 'Lord, Lord,' will enter the kingdom of heaven, but only the one who does the will of my Father who is in heaven."

In fact, because of the way Elisha handled the revival that was bequeathed to him, hunger was still in the land while he was still alive (2 Kings 8:1). This famine was to last for seven years. If the land had been cleaned of sin, would God have decreed a famine?

Chapter Four: The Earth Currently is Worse than the Time of Elisha

Asking for a double anointing in our present day will be as useless as that from Elijah to Elisha. At least there could just be performance of many miracles as Elisha did. God is looking for men who will be ahead of their generation. This generation is much more degenerative than the Israel that Elisha faced. In 1999, I was offered an Alexander von Humboldt Fellowship in Germany. On reaching there, I felt like returning back home immediately. The first thing that put me off was the way women dressed, in vulgar trousers. I felt that the world was coming to an end. I saw automatic doors. That reminded me about the book of revelation where it was stated that if you did not carry the number 666 you wouldn't be able to open any door including transaction of businesses.

"Here is wisdom. Let him who has understanding calculate the number of the beast, for the number is that of a man; and his number is six hundred and sixty-six" (Revelation 13:8).

I called my wife immediately and told her my experience.

I informed her that as an undergraduate at University of Nigeria, Nsukka, some two girls would put on trousers but the dresses were not vulgar; and yet the entire class would burst out in whistling until they became uncomfortable and they would stop using their trousers until about a year later. This continued until they became ashamed of themselves. Their pair of trousers were like those Indian type that is bogus and not revealing. Today in Nigeria, any woman who does not wear trousers is considered uncivilized to the extent that villagers have joined the group of trouser wearers. What a world! Even so-called Christian schools are worse. Their girls wear very vulgar and revealing trousers. The only school, I think, I have not seen any girl wearing any trouser is the Christian school called Bingham University, here in

Abuja, although I have not visited other schools.

Today, during this era of Covid-19, people are talking about a vaccine and a chip that will make people to be noticed wherever they are. In fact, automatic doors will respond easier to them so they can enter and purchase whatever they want. This era is worse than what I experienced in 1999, just about 21 years ago! Those who understand it are kicking against it but they are bowing to the devil in another area of their lives.

The Organogram of God

The earth, as it is, is in an order or organogram set by God. Distorting that organogram will automatically bring in God's judgment. You cannot disorganize God's order. In Europe, you can see a fiery preacher, that we in Nigeria will call a "great" man of God, introducing someone as his girlfriend! What a taboo! There is no "great" man of God in the Bible anyway. The other day, I saw on the net, a woman looking very happy, that she was pregnant for a gorilla since the population of gorillas were diminishing! This could have not happened in Elisha's Israel and the woman be allowed to live. She would have been roasted alive!

There are other forms of bestiality. As an Alexander von Humboldt Fellow in Germany, a dog jumped at me from a lady's hand. When I came back, I complained to my Moroccan neighbour about my encounter with the woman and her dog. He simply told me that the dog was aggressive towards me because "he" was the husband to the lady. Sleeping with animals would attract quick death penalty in those days. Today women who sleep with dogs and other beasts advertise themselves online! The world is upside down. The organogram of the earth is completely distorted! We hear of genetic engineering and recombinant DNA technology where various species are cross-matched including those of humans with animals and various animals with other species. We hear of gay marriages, oral sex and using toys as sex mates. We hear of stem cell research. What a world! In some countries, women feel that they are even superior to men and as such, many are not married. God's organogram is being toyed with by those men and women who claim they are intelligent. They should remember the Tower of Babel (Genesis 11). It is those toys that they are inventing that make them to think they are too much. Paul made the organogram very clear in 1 Corinthians 11: 3

"But I want you to realize that the head of every man

is Christ, and the head of the woman is man, and the head of Christ is God."

Today, the above organogram is distorted. Does it shock you that boys now use braided hair? Even men no longer have confidence in themselves so they behave like women. That is why men are now perming their hair.

The Origin of Islamic Militant Groups

The Double Anointing of Elisha

God has warned the world through various means. There are tornadoes, earth quakes, tsunamis, etc., all over the world. Many do not listen. Islamic State in Syria (ISIS) and Islamic State of West African Province, Al-Shabab, Al-Qaeda, Al-Nusra, Taliban, Boko Haram, name it, all came to warn man; perhaps he would turn back. Man does not want to listen. Isaiah 46:9-11 had this to say:

"Remember the former things, those of long ago; I am God, and there is no other; I am God, and there is none like me. I make known the end from the beginning, from ancient times, what is still to come. I say, 'My purpose will stand, and I will do all that I please.' From the east I summon a bird of prey; from a far-off land, a man to fulfill my purpose. What I have said, that I will

bring about; what I have planned, that I will do."

This is God's warning us. You cannot change God's counsel. You cannot change his purpose. Some will say, "How can God use ISIS and allied people?" He is saying here that He can use birds of prey. Birds of prey are ravenous birds and are regarded as unclean. He can use them to execute His counsel. God can use unholy people to bring His purpose to come to pass.

According to the Levitical law, birds of prey such as the eagle, the vulture, the hawk, etc., should not be eaten (Leviticus 14: 11-18). They are unclean. God can use anything to execute his purpose. When the children of Israel sinned, he used their enemies to torment them. Those enemies were not children of God.

I have read with interest that the current flu was not the first. Good as that sounds, were people living the way they are living today? In fact, most of those flus brought revival. Today, with the current flu, people will even live worse than they are doing now. If there has been flus in the past with lots of death, was the earth as degenerate as it is now? Look at the angle of the part of the earth that the flu had hit the highest. Those countries that have been hit hardest are those who claim that religion, particularly Christianity, is a mistake. In fact, they think that science is everything just because of the few toys they have been able to produce from God's creatures. Some countries believe that the Bible is just the folktales of the Hebrews.

In 1999, we visited a city called Magdeburg in Germany. Our tour guide told us that that was the city with the highest number of Christians in the country. He was even bold to tell us that Germans no longer believed in God. When he said that there many Christians in that city, I was very eager to hear the millions or thousands of people that were Christians in the city, only to hear that there were just 24 Protestants and 4 Catholics! He added that the large number of Protestants was because Magdeburg was only a 100 kilometres from Halle-Wittenberg where Martin Luther started his reformation. We visited a monastery in that city and the guide again told us that the 4 Catholics had bought back the monastery from the Government but only meat pie and some other food stuff were sold at the entrance while the inner portion was let out to actors from America and other places where they come to act films! He was only trying to say he did not believe in God because I know many German cities have many more Christians than those numbers the guide quoted.

The Double Anointing of Elisha

Do you wonder if the current Covid-19 hits some nations harder than others? Remember there are countries in Africa who have not so degenerated as much as those in the West, and only few of them have died from the current pestilence. That should teach us a bunch of lessons. If you are a preacher today, will the double anointing as requested by Elisha, be enough for you? Each generation has its challenges. The ones of nowadays are so much that asking God for a mere double anointing is useless. God is willing to let His children remain ahead of their generations. These are days when people are afraid of presenting the truth as they should. In most advanced countries, they will simply write beautiful stories and then tell you their people will understand. Many of the Christian magazines from the West are just beautiful stories that can only warm the mind but cannot convict anyone of sin.

Ask for Something More

We must not just be asking for double anointing like Elisha. Your double anointing may just be sufficient for miracles and nothing more. If Elisha on seeing the happenings of his time could ask for double the anointing of his master, won't you ask for anointing to keep you ahead of your generation? Remember that apart from the multiplication of the problems of the earth through people, Satan himself is on the prowl more than ever before. The Bible enjoins us in 1 Peter 5:8 that:

"Be sober, be vigilant; because your adversary the devil, as a roaring lion, walks about, seeking whom he may devour."

If Peter could write this in his generation, the situation has worsened more than his generation. When you look left, you see evil, when you turn right, you see evil, when you look straight, you see evil and when you look backwards, you also see evil. This is the time to look upwards to ask for God's help. In fact, some holiness preachers will tell you never to shake a woman or even when you greet them, you should look away from their eyes. Satan is not just in evil women but even in a place where no one is, he is there.

Who was in the Garden of Eden when he caused Adam and Eve to fall? The Bible recorded that when Adam and Eve fell in the Garden of Eden, God put a flaming swinging sword at the gate of the Garden (Genesis 3: 24).

"After he drove the man out, he placed on the east side of the Garden of Eden cherubim and a flaming sword flashing back and forth to guard the way to the tree of life."

This means that the Garden of Eden was an enclosure. Anywhere you are, Satan can reach you. It is therefore, unnecessary to be looking for anointing that keeps you from the common sins of everyday. It is time to ask for anointing to keep you far ahead of your generation and their desires and activities - to be able to pull them out of their sins. The type of anointing that makes one untouchable to the forces of darkness; whether alone or in the multitude. The battle is the Lords. Do not look at the strength of men. Do not look at what any man of God can achieve through miracles or prophesy. Such activities may only be helpful in the present generation. For every generation, God can have an anointing that can conquer that generation, if he has the man who qualifies for it. Do not think that every man is useful in God's hand. When the children of Israel were suffering in Egypt, God was waiting for one Moses to be well discipled by the conditions of life and his in-law, Jethro. He was to learn patience through the keeping of animals and life in his in law's house. God had promised Abraham that his children would go to a strange land for 400 years (Genesis 15:3). Yet, al the end of the 400 years, there seemed to be no body that was ready to be used. The came out after 430 years only when Moses was fully ready! (Exodus 12:40):

"Now the length of time the Israelite people lived in Egypt was 430 years."

God is not looking for just any man but the man that will not easily crumble under the weight of life's problems.

Chapter 5: Epilogue: You Can Finish Well

The best prayer any man can pray is the prayer to

finish well. Great men of God like Abraham, David, Moses, Aaron and a host of others could not finish well without a dent in their walk with God. For Abraham, it was the case of impregnating his maid, Hagar, without raising an altar to ask God (Genesis 16:4). Today the damage the children of the bond woman are doing to the earth is a painful one. For David, it was in the case of Bathsheba (2 Samuel 11:1-

5). For Moses he struck the rock the second time instead of speaking to the rock (Numbers 20:11). For Aaron it was in the case of the golden calf (Exodus 32:1-6). Anything that God said people should not do, is what men have love for. In our generation everything that God said people should not do, is what is reigning now. Naturally, it is in the nature of man to do the opposite of whatever God said man should not do.

The Double Anointing of Elisha

When God made man He told him to increase and multiply and to dominate the earth (Genesis 2:26). When men reached Babel, they told themselves to build a tower, in case they scatter on the face of the earth (Genies 11:1-9). The result is the multiple languages and tribes that are causing us trouble today. Meanwhile, God's intention was for men to scatter so that wild animals will not out grow them and begin to kill them.

When Jesus was about to leave to heaven, He told His disciples to preach the gospel from Jerusalem to Judea and to the uttermost parts of the earth (Acts 1: 8). When He left, the disciples were not ready to reach the rest of the world until persecution came and people like James were killed (Acts 12: 2).

Today, there are too many things that God commanded that men should not do, but they are now reigning and even Christians are practicing them without bothering about the consequences. One of such is the use of tattoo. The Bible recorded that no man should tattoo his body (Leviticus 19:28).

"Do not cut your bodies for the dead or put tattoo marks on yourselves. I am the LORD."

Yet this is what is reigning now. It is in the nature of man to act against whatever God says. I can continue to recount on and on several things that God said we should not do. Instead of pointing out those faults, such as wearing of men's clothes by women, covering of the heard during prayers, let me go to the issue of asking God for anointing sufficient enough not to join them. It is going to take Christians energy to refrain from these activities as the days become shorter and shorter for the return of Jesus Christ. After all, many will argue, some women are putting on these attitudes and are doing well in the house of God; some even as pastors. What you call doing well are your definitions and not God's. Every Christian must ask God clearly before joining any group. The aim of every Christian is to finish well. Do not allow the world to attract you.

"For everything in the world--the lust of the flesh, the lust of the eyes, and the pride of life--comes not from the Father but from the world" (1 John 2:16).

Do not allow what you see in the world to finish your journey to heaven. The world was not created by God. The world and its system is the creation of the evil one. The earth was created by God. Thus, the earth is in the grip of our Lord God. The world is in the grips of the evil one. The Bible said in 1 John 5:19:

"We know that we are children of God, and that the whole world is under the control of the evil one."

For you to finish well and finish strong you must hate the world as much as possible; be they the world of sports, the world of music and so and so forth. We must always know there are two divides: the world of God and the world systems. The two are not compatible. You cannot love God and say you love the world.

I have stated earlier that every man that God uses, He passes him through some tests. One of the tests is that He passes the man through a zig-zag road. On that road, you will find the men, the materials and sometimes the money you need to persecute God's work. For many people who faint along "this road" they jump the steps God wants them to take. Many have their eyes on the money for the ministry. That is actually the least of what God needs His followers to have. May God help us to be patient so that the formation He wants us to have that will make us real heavenly minded people will come to us. May we be heavenly minded. And, may we finish strong.

Michael Adikwu

The Double Anointing of Elisha

Michael Adikwu

The Double Anointing of Elisha

www.ingramcontent.com/pod-product-compliance
Lightning Source LLC
Chambersburg PA
CBHW072020110526
44592CB00012B/1388